Travel Journal

Alaska

VPJournals

ISBN-13: 978-1518843938
ISBN-10: 151884393X

Contact Details

Name: _____

Email address: _____

Tel: _____

Address: _____

_____

_____

Important Medical Information

Blood type: _____

Medication: _____

CONTENTS

Hi, I hope you enjoy this journal. It is packed with cool stuff and recommendations for you trip to Alaska, and has plenty of space to record details of your trip.

Have fun in Alaska!

Great Places to visit in Alaska

Alaska Museum of Natural History	✓
Alaska Wildlife Conservation Center	
Eagle River Nature Center	
Alaska Highway	
Wrangell-St. Elias National Park	
Iditarod National Historic Trail	
Seward, Alaska	
Totem Bight State Historic Park	
Mendenhall Glacier	
Arctic Circle Tours	
Klondike Gold Rush National Historical Park	
Harding Icefield	

Kenai Fjords National Park	
Tony Knowles Coastal Trail	
Seward's Exit Glacier	
Homer Spit	
Chena Riverwalk	
Little Campbell Lake	
Georgeson Botanical Garden	
Gobblers Knob	
Mount Aurora Skiland	
Wynn Nature Center	
Add your own after researching	

Cool Places to visit in Alaska with Kids

Elmendorf State Fish Hatchery	✓
Alaska Native Heritage Center	
Alaska Wildlife Conservation Center	
H2Oasis Waterpark	
Begich Boggs Visitor Center	
Tracy Arm Fjord	
Kenai Fjords National Park	
Iditarod National Historic Trail	
Alaska Wild Berry Products	
The Reindeer Farm	
Anchorage Museum	
Fountainhead Antique Auto Museum	

St Elias Mountains	
Alaska SeaLife Center	
Juneau Icefield	
Alaska Range	
Inside Passage	
University of Alaska Museum of the North	
Anchorage Museum of Art and History	
Alaska State Museum	
Kincaid Sand Dunes	
Denali National Park	
Add your own after researching	

Good Places to Eat in Alaska

Moose's Tooth Pub and Pizzeria	✓
Kincaid Grill and Wine Bar	
Great Harvest Bread Co	
Snow City Cafe	
Jens' Restaurant	
Glacier Brewhouse	
Bear Tooth Theatrepub & Grill	
Sacks Cafe and Restaurant	
Tommy's Burger Stop	
Fire Island Rustic Bakeshop	
Pita Place	
Bad 2 Da Bone	

The Crepery	
Lavelle's Bistro	
Chena's Alaskan Grill	
Thai House Restaurant	
Lemon Grass Thai Cuisine	
Wasabi Bay	
Mc Cafferty's A Coffee House	
Cookie Jar Restaurant	
Krazy Moose Subs	
The Grape Tap	
Add your own after researching	

Best Websites to Research Further

Do some more research on the internet to plan your trip:

www.wikipedia.org/wiki/Alaska
www.TravelAlaska.com
www.anchorage.net
www.alaska.gov
www.alaska.org
www.awesomeamerica.com/Alaska
www.AlaskaTravel.com
www.lonelyplanet.com/usa/alaska
www.Alaskaone.com
www.wikitravel.org/Alaska

More places I want to visit on our trip

1. _____

2. _____

3. _____

4. _____

5. _____

6. _____

7. _____

8. _____

9. _____

10. _____

11. _____

12. _____

13. _____

14. _____

15. _____

Postcard List

Name:
Address:

Name:
Address:

Name:
Address:

Name:

Address:

Name:

Address:

Name:

Address:

Name:

Address:

Name:

Address:

Name:

Address:

Name:

Address:

Name:

Address:

Name:

Address:

Name:

Address:

Name:

Address:

MAIL

Packing List

✓	This Journal
	Tickets
	Passport
	Money
	Chargers
	Batteries
	Book to read
	Camera
	Tablet
	Sun glasses
	Sun cream

	Toiletries
	Water
	Watch
	Snacks
	Umbrella
	Towel
	Guide book
	Kindle
	Jacket
	Medication
	Add more below

Alaska Facts

- The name Alaska is derived from the Aleut word "Aleyska," meaning "great land"

- Alaska is the largest state in the US, 1/5 of the entire USA and is twice as big as Texas

- There are places in Alaska that get 24 hours of sunlight, and places that get 24 hours of darkness

- Alaska has over 3 million lakes and 130 volcanoes

- Alaska has an estimated 100,000 glaciers, ranging from tiny cirque glaciers to huge valley glaciers

- Alaskan Kodiak and Polar Bears can grow to 1,400 pounds and 11 feet tall. Moose can grow to 1,350 pounds, 5 feet high to shoulder with an antlers span of 72 inches

- The Pribilof Islands area is home to around 1 million seals and 2.5m birds

- Juneau has no road access to the rest of the state. It is the only capital city in the United States accessible only by boat or plane. It is also the largest U.S. city covering 3,108 square miles.

- In 1926 13-year-old Bennie Benson from Cognac, Alaska designed the state flag.

- Of the 20 highest peaks in the United States, 17 are in Alaska. Mt. McKinley, the highest peak in North America, is 20,320 ft. above sea level. Denali, the Indian name for the peak, means "The Great One."

- Three groups of natives lived in Alaska: Eskimos, Aleuts, and Indians.

- Aurora Borealis [northern lights] can be seen an average of 243 days a year in FairBanks. The northern lights are produced by charged electrons and protons striking the earth's upper atmosphere.

- During the Klondike gold rush in 1897, potatoes were so highly valued for their vitamin C content, that miners traded gold for them.

Clothes & Shoe Sizes

Children's Shoe Sizes

UK	EUROPE	US	Japan
4	20	4½ or 5	12 ½
4 ½	21	5 or 5½	13
5	21 or 22	5½ or 6	13 ½
5 ½	22	6	13½ or 14
6	23	6½ or 7	14 or 14½
6 ½	23 or 24	7 ½	14½ or 15
7	24	7½ or 8	15
7 ½	25	8 or 9	15 ½
8	25 or 26	8½ or 9	16
8 ½	26	9½	16 ½
9	27	9½ or 10	16 ½ or 17
10	28	10½ or 11	17 ½
10½ or 11	29	11½ or 12	18
11 ½	30	12½	18 or 18 ½
12	31	13	19 or 19 ½
12 ½	31	13 or 13½	19 ½ or 20
13	32	1	20
13 ½	32 ½	1 ½	20 ½
1	33	1½ or 2	21
2	34	2½ or 3	22

Children's Clothing Sizes

UK	EUROPE	US	Australia
12m	80cm	12-18m	12m
18m	80-86cm	18-24m	18m
24m	86-92cm	23-24m	2
2-3	92-98cm	2T	3
3-4	98-104cm	4T	4
3-5	104-110cm	5	5
5-6	110-116cm	6	6
6-7	116-122cm	6X-7	7
7-8	122-128cm	7 to 8	8
8-9	128-134cm	9 to 10	9
9-10	134-140cm	10	10
10-11	140-146cm	11	11
11-12	146-152cm	14	12

Women's Shoe Sizes

UK	EUROPE	US	Japan
3	35 ½	5	22 ½
3 ½	36	5 ½	23
4	37	6	23
4 ½	37 ½	6 ½	23 ½
5	38	7	24
5 ½	39	7 ½	24
6	39 ½	8	24 ½
6 ½	40	8 ½	25
7	41	9 ½	25 ½
7 ½	41 ½	10	26
8	42	10 ½	26 ½

Women's Clothes Sizes

UK	US	Japan	France / Spain	Germany	Italy	Australia
6/8	6	7-9	36	34	40	8
10	8	9-11	38	36	42	10
12	10	11-13	40	38	44	12
14	12	13-15	42	39	46	14
16	14	15-17	44	40	48	16
18	16	17-19	46	42	50	18
20	18	19-21	48	44	52	20

Men's Shoe Sizes

UK	EUROPE	US	Japan
6	38 ½	6 ½	24 ½
6 ½	39	7	25
7	40	7 ½	25 ½
7 ½	41	8	26
8	42	8 ½	27 ½
8 ½	43	9	27 ½
9	43 ½	9 ½	28
9 ½	44	10	28 ½
10	44	10 ½	28 ½
10 ½	44 ½	11	29
11	45	12	29 ½

Men's Suit / Coat / Sweater Sizes

UK / US / Aus	EU / Japan	General
32	42	Small
34	44	Small
36	46	Small
38	48	Medium
40	50	Large
42	52	Large
44	54	Extra Large
46	56	Extra Large

Men's Pants / Trouser Sizes (Waist)

UK / US	Europe
32	81 cm
34	86 cm
36	91 cm
38	97 cm
40	102 cm
42	107 cm

We have included another copy of this at the back of the book, so you can find it quickly again when you are in Alaska

Alaska Trip Diary

Write a daily diary during your trip

Day 1

Date: _____   **Weather:** _____

_____

_____

_____

_____

_____

_____

_____

_____

_____

_____

_____

_____

_____

Day 2

Date: _____   **Weather:** _____

_____

_____

_____

_____

_____

_____

_____

_____

_____

_____

_____

_____

_____

Day 3

Date: _____   **Weather:** _____

Day 4

Date: _____   **Weather:** _____

_____

_____

_____

_____

_____

_____

_____

_____

_____

_____

_____

_____

_____

_____

Day 5

Date: _____   **Weather:** _____

_____

_____

_____

_____

_____

_____

_____

_____

_____

_____

_____

_____

_____

_____

_____

_____

Day 6

Date: _____   **Weather:** _____

Day 7

Date: _____   **Weather:** _____

Day 8

Date: _____   **Weather:** _____

_____

_____

_____

_____

_____

_____

_____

_____

_____

_____

_____

_____

_____

Day 9

Date: _____   **Weather:** _____

_____

_____

_____

_____

_____

_____

_____

_____

_____

_____

_____

_____

_____

_____

Day 10

Date: _____   **Weather:** _____

_____

_____

_____

_____

_____

_____

_____

_____

_____

_____

_____

_____

_____

_____

Day 11

Date: _____   **Weather:** _____

Day 12

Date: _____   Weather: _____

Day 13

Date: _____   **Weather:** _____

Day 14

Date: _____   **Weather:** _____

_____

_____

_____

_____

_____

_____

_____

_____

_____

_____

_____

_____

_____

_____

Day 15

Date: _____   **Weather:** _____

Day 16

Date: _____   **Weather:** _____

_____

_____

_____

_____

_____

_____

_____

_____

_____

_____

_____

_____

_____

_____

_____

Day 17

Date: _____   **Weather:** _____

_____

_____

_____

_____

_____

_____

_____

_____

_____

_____

_____

_____

_____

_____

_____

_____

_____

Day 18

Date: _____   **Weather:** _____

Day 19

Date: _____   **Weather:** _____

Day 20

Date: _____   **Weather:** _____

Day 21

Date: _____   **Weather:** _____

Memories of your Trip

Things I will remember from the trip

Favorite Places visited on the Trip

People I Met

Name:
Address:
Tel:
email:

Name:
Address:
Tel:
email:

Name:
Address:
Tel:
email:

Name:
Address:
Tel:
email:

Name:
Address:
Tel:
email:

Name:
Address:
Tel:
email:

Name:
Address:
Tel:
email:

Name:
Address:
Tel:
email:

Name:
Address:
Tel:
email:

Name:
Address:
Tel:
email:

Name:
Address:
Tel:
email:

We hope you enjoyed your trip to Alaska

Please leave us a review if you found this Journal useful

Check out our useful resources on the next few pages

Clothes & Shoe Sizes

Children's Shoe Sizes

UK	EUROPE	US	Japan
4	20	4½ or 5	12 ½
4 ½	21	5 or 5½	13
5	21 or 22	5½ or 6	13 ½
5 ½	22	6	13½ or 14
6	23	6½ or 7	14 or 14½
6 ½	23 or 24	7 ½	14½ or 15
7	24	7½ or 8	15
7 ½	25	8 or 9	15 ½
8	25 or 26	8½ or 9	16
8 ½	26	9½	16 ½
9	27	9½ or 10	16 ½ or 17
10	28	10½ or 11	17 ½
10½ or 11	29	11½ or 12	18
11 ½	30	12½	18 or 18 ½
12	31	13	19 or 19 ½
12 ½	31	13 or 13½	19 ½ or 20
13	32	1	20
13 ½	32 ½	1 ½	20 ½
1	33	1½ or 2	21
2	34	2½ or 3	22

Children's Clothing Sizes

UK	EUROPE	US	Australia
12m	80cm	12-18m	12m
18m	80-86cm	18-24m	18m
24m	86-92cm	23-24m	2
2-3	92-98cm	2T	3
3-4	98-104cm	4T	4
3-5	104-110cm	5	5
5-6	110-116cm	6	6
6-7	116-122cm	6X-7	7
7-8	122-128cm	7 to 8	8
8-9	128-134cm	9 to 10	9
9-10	134-140cm	10	10
10-11	140-146cm	11	11
11-12	146-152cm	14	12

Women's Shoe Sizes

UK	EUROPE	US	Japan
3	35 ½	5	22 ½
3 ½	36	5 ½	23
4	37	6	23
4 ½	37 ½	6 ½	23 ½
5	38	7	24
5 ½	39	7 ½	24
6	39 ½	8	24 ½
6 ½	40	8 ½	25
7	41	9 ½	25 ½
7 ½	41 ½	10	26
8	42	10 ½	26 ½

Women's Clothes Sizes

UK	US	Japan	France / Spain	Germany	Italy	Australia
6/8	6	7-9	36	34	40	8
10	8	9-11	38	36	42	10
12	10	11-13	40	38	44	12
14	12	13-15	42	39	46	14
16	14	15-17	44	40	48	16
18	16	17-19	46	42	50	18
20	18	19-21	48	44	52	20

Men's Shoe Sizes

UK	EUROPE	US	Japan
6	38 ½	6 ½	24 ½
6 ½	39	7	25
7	40	7 ½	25 ½
7 ½	41	8	26
8	42	8 ½	27 ½
8 ½	43	9	27 ½
9	43 ½	9 ½	28
9 ½	44	10	28 ½
10	44	10 ½	28 ½
10 ½	44 ½	11	29
11	45	12	29 ½

Men's Suit / Coat / Sweater Sizes

UK / US / Aus	EU / Japan	General
32	42	Small
34	44	Small
36	46	Small
38	48	Medium
40	50	Large
42	52	Large
44	54	Extra Large
46	56	Extra Large

Men's Pants / Trouser Sizes (Waist)

UK / US	Europe
32	81 cm
34	86 cm
36	91 cm
38	97 cm
40	102 cm
42	107 cm

Common Translations

English	French	Spanish	Italian
Hello	Bonjour	Hola	Ciao
Goodbye	Au revoir	Adiós	Arrivederci
Yes	Oui	Sí	Si
No	Non	No	No
Please	S'il-vous-plaît	Por favor	Per favore
Thank you	Merci	Gracias	Grazie
Excuse me	Excusez-moi	Perdón	Mi scusi
How much	Combien	Cuánto	Quanto
My name is	Mon nom est	Mi nombre es	Io mi chiamo
Where is	Où est	Dónde está	Dov'è
The bank	La banque	El banco	La banca
The toilet	Les toilettes	El baño	Il bagno

German	Japanese	Mandarin	Hindi
Hallo	Kon'nichiwa	Ni hao	Namaste
Auf Wiedersehen	Sayonara	Zaijian	Alavida
Ja	Hai	Shi de	Ham
Nein	Ie	Meiyou	Nahim
Bitte	Onegaishimasu	Qing	Krpaya
Vielen Dank	Arigato	Xiexie	Dhan'yavada
Entschuldigung	Sumimasen	Duoshao	Mujhe mapha karem
Wie viel	Ikura	Wo de mingzi shi	Kitana
Mein Name ist	Watashinonamaeha	Nali	Mera nama hai
Wo ist	Doko ni aru	Yinhang	Kaham hai
Die Bank	Ginko	Yinhang	Bainka
Die Toilette	Toire	Cesuo	Saucalaya

Notes:

51170906R00078

Made in the USA
San Bernardino, CA
14 July 2017